THE NORTH POLE

Arctic Circle

RUSSIA

Laptev Sea

ARCTIC OCEAN

╋ **North Pole**

Queen Elizabeth Islands

Baffin Bay

GREENLAND

Denmark Strait

By Todd Bluthenthal

Gareth Stevens
PUBLISHING

Please visit our website, www.garethstevens.com. For a free color catalog of all our high-quality books, call toll free 1-800-542-2595 or fax 1-877-542-2596.

Cataloging-in-Publication Data

Names: Bluthenthal, Todd.
Title: The North Pole / Todd Bluthenthal.
Description: New York : Gareth Stevens Publishing, 2018. | Series: Where on Earth? mapping parts of the world | Includes index.
Identifiers: ISBN 9781482464290 (pbk.) | ISBN 9781482464313 (library bound) | ISBN 9781482464306 (6 pack)
Subjects: LCSH: Arctic regions–Juvenile literature. | North Pole–Juvenile literature.
Classification: LCC GN673.B58 2017 | DDC 971.9–dc23

Published in 2018 by
Gareth Stevens Publishing
111 East 14th Street, Suite 349
New York, NY 10003

Designer: Samantha DeMartin
Editor: Joan Stoltman

Photo credits: series art CHAPLIA YAROSLAV/Shutterstock.com; cover, p. 1 (map) Rainer Lesniewski/Shutterstock.com; cover, p. 1 (photo) Denis Burdin/Shutterstock.com; pp. 5, 13, 19 Maksimilian/Shutterstock.com; p. 7 Istimages/Shutterstock.com; p. 9 (top) Milagli/Shutterstock.com; p. 9 (bottom) outdoorsman/Shutterstock.com; pp. 11, 15, 17 Peter Hermes Furian/Shutterstock.com; p. 21 Ansgar Walk/Wikimedia Commons.

Printed in the United States of America

CPSIA compliance information: Batch #CS17GS: For further information contact Gareth Stevens, New York, New York at 1-800-542-2595.

CONTENTS

Boldface words appear in the glossary.

What Is the North Pole?

The North Pole is the northernmost point of Earth. That means everything else on Earth is south of the North Pole! It's found at **latitude** 90° north. The North Pole isn't on land. It's in the Arctic Ocean!

The imaginary lines that make up Earth's **time zones** all meet at the North Pole. That means the North Pole is in every time zone at once! All the lines of **longitude** also meet at the North Pole.

▽ 3910 North Pole

ARCTIC OCEAN

Two North Poles!

There are two North Poles! The magnetic North Pole is the spot on Earth that **compasses** point to when they point north. It's always moving! Right now, it's on Ellesmere Island in Canada, 500 miles (800 km) south of the North Pole!

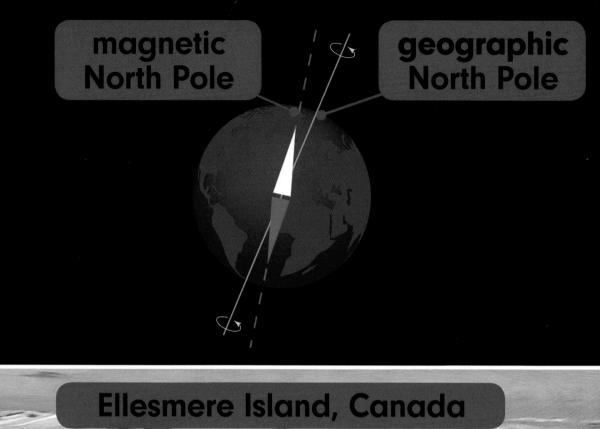

magnetic North Pole

geographic North Pole

Ellesmere Island, Canada

9

What Is the Arctic?

The North Pole is in the Arctic. The Arctic is the area north of the **Arctic Circle** on a map. Some land belonging to North America, Europe, and Asia is inside the Arctic Circle. However, the North Pole and the Arctic Ocean aren't part of any country!

The sea around the North Pole is covered in ice and snow, which makes it look like land. However, the nearest land is hundreds of miles away! Arctic sea ice can be anywhere from 10 feet (3 m) thick to 100 feet (30 m) thick.

What's It Like at the North Pole?

The North Pole has sunlight all day and night in summer, and no sunlight at all in winter. This is because Earth's **axis** is **tilted** and because of the way Earth moves around the sun.

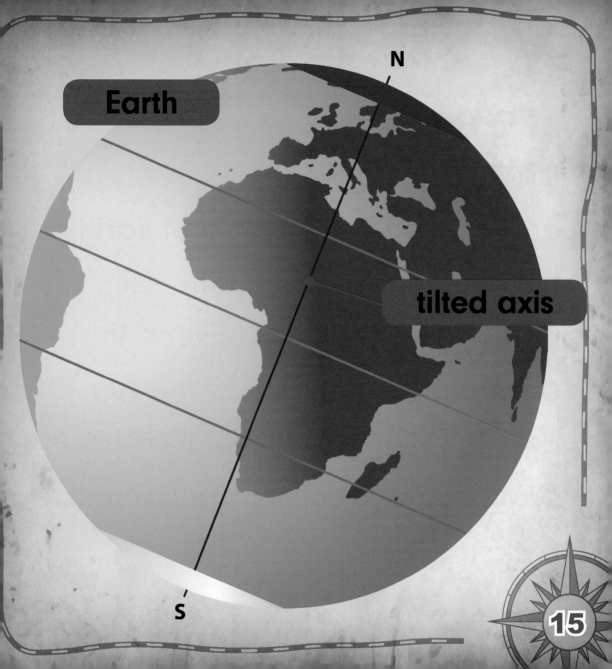

N

Earth

tilted axis

S

15

It takes Earth 1 year to move around the sun. Because of Earth's tilt, different parts face the sun at different times of the year. In summer, the Arctic faces the sun day and night! In winter, it faces away from the sun day and night!

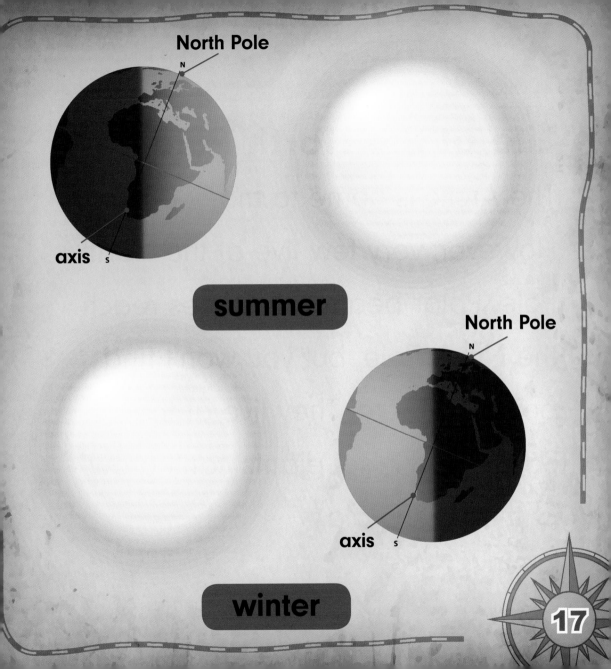

North Pole

axis

summer

North Pole

axis

winter

17

Life at the North Pole

The Arctic is home to many animals. However, very few live at the North Pole. Polar bears sometimes reach the North Pole, but you won't find penguins there. They live at the South Pole! Also, plants can't grow at the North Pole.

Few people have visited the North Pole. Some people do live inside the Arctic Circle, though! The Inuit and Yupik peoples have lived there for thousands of years! Alert, Canada, is the community closest to the North Pole. It's nearly 500 miles (800 km) away!

Inuit

GLOSSARY

Arctic Circle: an imaginary line that circles the northernmost parts of Earth

axis: an imaginary straight line around which a planet turns

compass: a tool for finding directions

geographic: having to do with the study of Earth and its features

latitude: the imaginary lines on maps that run east and west

longitude: the imaginary lines on maps that run north and south

tilted: slanted, not straight up and down

time zone: a geographic area inside which a standard time is used. Earth is divided into 24 time zones.

FOR MORE INFORMATION

BOOKS

Besel, Jennifer M. *The Coldest Places on Earth.* Mankato, MN: Capstone Press, 2010.

Parker, Victoria. *How Far Is Far? Comparing Geographical Distances.* Chicago, IL: Heinemann Library, 2011.

Waldron, Melanie. *Polar Regions.* Chicago, IL: Raintree, 2013.

WEBSITES

The Arctic: Facts
activewild.com/the-arctic-facts-for-kids/
Read all about the Arctic, its animals, its plants, and more!

North Pole Video
video.nationalgeographic.com/video/arctic_northpole
View an exciting video of the North Pole!

What's the Story? The Arctic
cbc.ca/kidscbc2/the-feed/whats-the-story-the-arctic
Learn more about the North Pole!

INDEX